JIŘÍ DVOŘÁK spent his childhood in Prague and wanted to become a botanist or the author of adventure novels. After graduating with a degree in plant biotechnology, he realized he did not want to be a scientist. He first worked as a proofreader and is now the editor-in-chief of the magazine *Our Beautiful Garden*. He is the author of more than ten books that combine his passions for biology and adventure. He has been awarded the Golden Ribbon, lives in Prague, and likes to take pictures, sleep, and be silent.

MARIE ŠTUMPFOVÁ graduated with a degree in graphics and illustration. Today, she mainly devotes herself to illustration, editorial work, and creating books. Her work as an art director can be seen in *Page* magazine, and she has also designed wooden toys for children. She created the book *How Animals Sleep* as her diploma thesis, which has received praise from critics and readers. Today, it can be read by children in Japan, Poland, Holland, Korea, Hungary, and now the English-speaking world. mariestumpfova.com

---

How Animals Sleep
This edition published in 2024 by Red Comet Press, LLC, Brooklyn, NY

First published as *Jak Zvířata Spi* • Original Czech text by Jiří Dvořák • Illustrations by Marie Štumpfová
© 2014 BAOBAB, Prague, Czech Republic • English translation © 2024 Red Comet Press, LLC • Translated by Benjamin Lovett

Library of Congress Control Number: 2023941968
ISBN (HB): 978-1-63655-097-8
ISBN (EBOOK): 978-1-63655-098-5

23 24 25 26 27 TLF 10 9 8 7 6 5 4 3 2 1

First Edition • Manufactured in China

RedCometPress.com

MIX
Paper | Supporting responsible forestry
FSC® C104723

HOW ANIMALS SLEEP

written by JIŘÍ DVOŘÁK   illustrations by MARIE ŠTUMPFOVÁ   translated by BENJAMIN LOVETT

RED COMET PRESS • BROOKLYN

PELICANS

Pelicans like company. Together, they fish, bask in the sun, and sleep. If they are unsure of their safety, one of them stays awake to keep watch. The others tuck their heads under their wings and fall asleep in the white darkness of pelican feathers.

PARROTFISH

Parrotfish live in warm, salty water
among the coral. Every night, they
build themselves a house—a bubble made
of their own saliva—to protect themselves
from predators. And when they awake,
they shake it off and rejoin a much
greater bubble. We might call it the sea.
Or the world.

BUMBLEBEES

Once a bumblebee leaves its nest, it never returns. During the day it drinks nectar and seeks out young queen bees. At night it finds a place to rest its wings. Sometimes it hides inside a flower—it is warmer there than outside. Other times it clings tightly to a blossom. Weary and stiff in the morning, it looks drained and ill. But it is only the chill of the night that has sapped its strength. When the morning grows warm, it will fly back to its sweet world once more. The sun recharges its batteries, just like it recharges ours.

SEA OTTERS

The sea otter spends most of its life in the water. It hunts, plays, and sleeps there. Rolling onto its back, it rests on the waves and clutches long strands of seaweed so the current will not carry it away. Mommy otter places her baby onto her belly and together the two close their eyes . . . Above them, stars peek through holes in their dark blanket, beneath them, their briny bed rocks them till morning.

SEALS

As if snuggling beneath a blanket, seals hide under the water when they want to sleep. They close their nostrils with a flap, so no water can get in, switch off half their brain, and just doze. Young seals wake to breathe every fifteen minutes, while grown-ups take a breath every half hour. Quick, gulp down the air, and be careful of polar bears! Then it's down again, back to the depths of sea and sleep. Back to the place they feel safe.

POLAR BEARS

Polar bears do not hibernate like brown bears. But they do sleep deeply when they need to. A mother bear who is expecting young will spend lots of time sleeping in her den. A bear caught in a blizzard will dig a hole and allow himself to be tucked in by the white blanket. A family, exhausted by a long swim at sea, will clamber up on an iceberg, take a nap, and gather strength for another journey. When winter passes, the icebergs will melt leaving the bears with fewer places to lay their heads.

FLAMINGOS

Flamingos sleep on one foot. Not to show off, but so they will not catch a chill in the cold water. They turn their heads into the breeze so that no raindrops drip beneath their quills. And like slender trees, they tower above the water, swaying in gusts of wind.

HAZEL DORMICE

No sooner does the hazel dormouse wake in the spring than it begins to dream of sleep. Straight away, it starts to make its grassy nests: one on a branch, one in a bird house, yet another in a hollow tree . . . It chooses one in which to bear its young, the other lairs are just for resting. Dormice live in almost every forest. So why have you not seen one yet? Because they sleep during the day and only leave their nests when we are climbing into ours. If ever you come across a velvety, rusty-coated creature asleep among the bushes in its grassy bed, be sure to stay as quiet as a dormouse. You do not want to wake him.

GIRAFFES

Giraffes do not get much sleep. And the two hours they get each night are broken up into small five-minute naps. After each one, they listen far out into the night for any sign of a lion on the prowl. Giraffes do have lots of dreams, however.

Short giraffe dreams. Dreams about juicy acacias, running on the savanna, cool shade at noon . . . And morning finds them with hooves on the ground, heads resting on the highest branches, and dreams just fading from memory.

CATS

Of all the domestic mammals, cats sleep the most. Sometimes as much as sixteen hours a day. They can fall asleep anywhere: on a chair, in a shoebox, or at the foot of a bed. By the time a cat has reached the ripe old age of nine, she has spent a mere three years of her life with open eyes. The rest of the time has been spent sleeping. Perhaps that is why cats begin having dreams the very first week they are born. Dreams in which mice are fatter, milk is creamier, and dogs do not know how to run. Not even greyhounds. Good night.

GREEN TREE PYTHONS

A green tree python sleeps the whole day through. It wraps itself twice around its branch, resting its head in the nest of its coils. No one notices it amidst the leaves in the green twilight of the jungle. At evening time, the python awakes. It flicks out its tail and waits to see who will take the bait. Anything that draws close enough is caught and swallowed. Then the serpent recoils itself around its branch, lays its head back in place, and falls asleep, one curious mouse fatter . . .

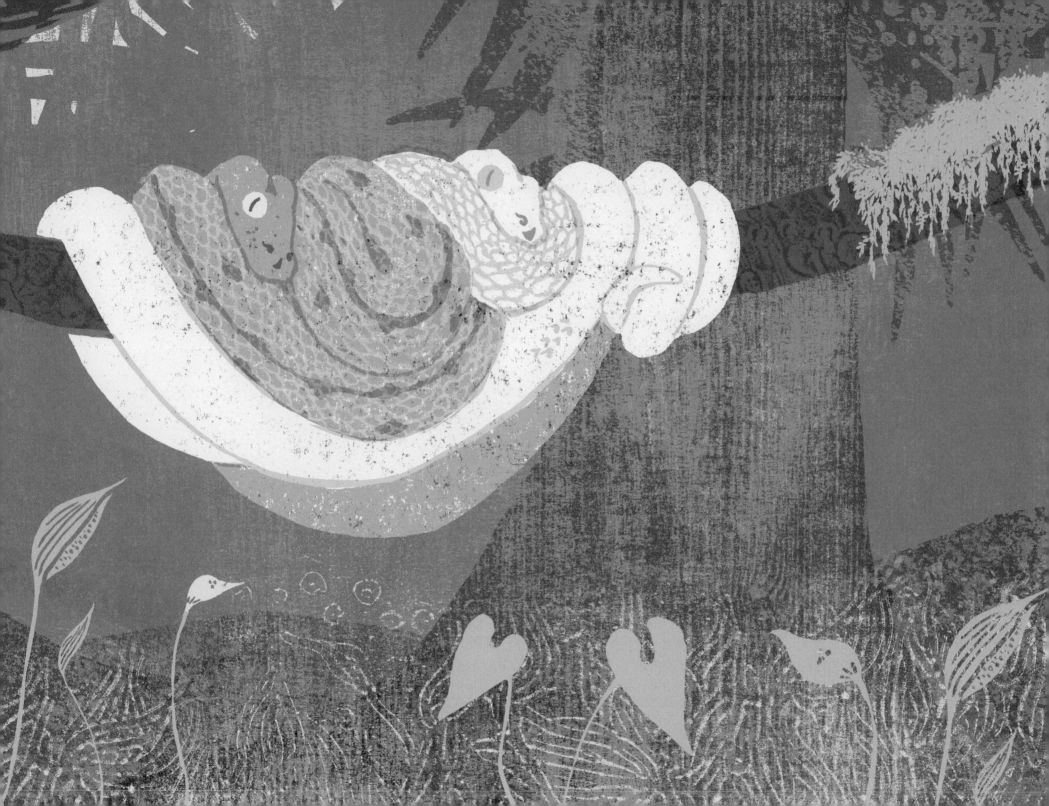

FOXES

Foxes often doze the day away in their dens, but they also like basking outside on sunny hillsides. Curled up in a little ball, their tails under their heads in place of a pillow, they close their eyes . . . There is plenty of time. They do not hunt till dusk. There are many foxes in our part of the world—in forest meadows, even parks. But we do not know they are there, for they are well hidden and do not much care for our company. Perhaps we are not clever enough.

We hardly sleep.

PEACOCKS

During the day, the peacock runs along the ground, enjoying the admiration of all. But come nightfall, it is glad to find its perch at the top of a tree. There it can rest, safe from foxes and wild dogs that could pounce on it in the darkness. Firmly clutching its branch, the peacock folds its tail, lowers its head, and falls asleep while a thousand eyes close all at once. Yet if it dreams, it is sure to have no more than one.

CAMELS

Whoever wants to sleep on the hot desert sand needs a sleeping pad, and perhaps a windbreaker. Camels have both. They do not sleep lying down, but kneel instead. Only their knees and elbows touch the sand, and these are protected by thick calluses, while the night breeze fans their bellies. By morning, the cold desert night has chilled the stores of fat they carry in their humps. Like icebergs on their backs, they will keep them cool in the baking desert heat. And now, once again, the time has come to set out for the oasis. Or is it a mirage? Camels are never mistaken, but people sometimes are . . .

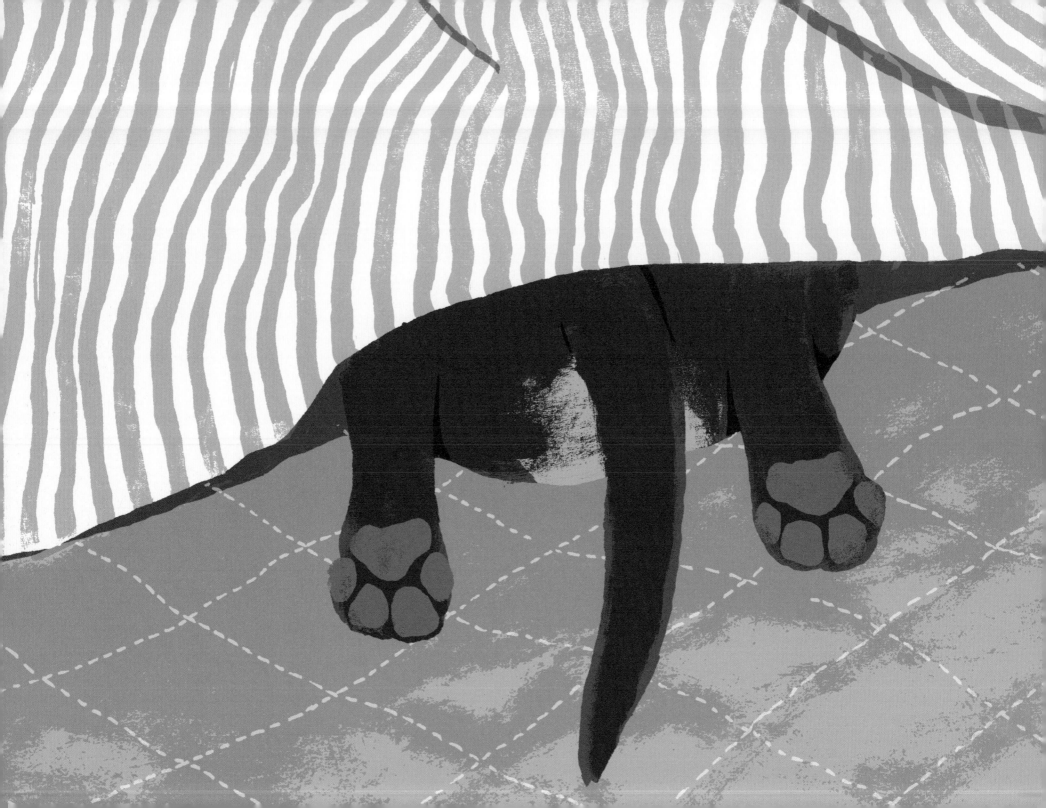

DOGS

If dogs sleep away the better part of the day, then puppies sleep away the best part. Yet they spend very little time immersed in the deep waters of sleep, usually wading knee-deep in slumber, eyes closed, but ears and nose gulping down the surrounding sounds and smells . . . Just in case. Dogs have dreams too. Everyone who has owned a dog knows that. And dogs know that too. They have even been known to gently wake a friend in the throes of a nightmare. Perhaps people learned that from them. Or the other way around.

COMMON SWIFTS

One eye open, one eye shut—that is how the swift sleeps. When night falls, the flock rises as high as it can into the sky. Then the birds spread their wings wide and gradually glide down to earth, hidden in darkness and slumber. One half of their brain sleeps, while the other half keeps watch, monitors their descent, and looks out for predators . . .

Young swifts spend two years in flight, only landing when it is time to build their nests. Then they begin a new life full of catching flies, twittering, pulled feathers, and sleepless nights.

HOW DO YOU SLEEP?

DO YOU REMEMBER YOUR DREAMS?

CAN YOU PRETEND TO SLEEP LIKE
THE ANIMALS IN THIS BOOK?

Free Education Guides and more at RedCometPress.com/Resources